D1572179

Nobody Told Me *that the* Road Would Be Easy

Devotions for People Working for Justice and Peace

FLOYD THOMPKINS JR.
EDITED BY TAMMY LAI

Nobody Told Me That the Road Would Be Easy

Devotions for People Working for Justice and Peace

Floyd Thompkins Jr.

Edited by Tammy Lai

ISBN (Print Edition): 978-1-66788-875-0

ISBN (eBook Edition): 978-1-66788-876-7

Contents

Foreword

SO often prayer and protest, contemplation and action, are divided to the detriment of the human soul. This is why the Rev. Floyd Thompkins, Jr., offers a gift to every human being, and not solely those working for justice and peace in the world. He calls every reader—young and old, male and female, prophet and priest, high church and low church and no church—to become whole in head, heart, and hands. He calls for activists, community organizers, preachers, teachers, and administrators of justice to wade into the waters of the Spirit and to worship the Wellspring of life and healing. These meaningful meditations beckon us to breathe the Breath and savor the Spirit in order to renew us for the work our souls must have.

The work should be rooted in worship therefore Thompkins calls us to worship each week and every day. By doing so, he wisely links worship and social witness. He resists bifurcations to receive the blessing of conjunctions and a more whole and honest reflection of life before God. To be clear, it is a life of both lament and hope. The title of this book—"nobody told me that the road would be easy"—is from a James Cleveland gospel song that also rings out, "I don't believe He brought me this far to leave me." There is struggle (e.g. "bullying and gaslighting") and there is hope (e.g. "the joy of God"). There is a yearning for both "the suffering servant and the risen Lord." Thompkins tells the truth while he trusts in the One who is ever present in the time of trouble. There's a rough road in social justice work but there's a deep sense of hope for redemption as well because of God's promise to never leave us nor forsake us.

Even through the lament, there's lots of love in the spiritual journey—a love for truth, a love for justice, a love for hope, and a love for all of God's children. Lament can be a gesture of love because it abhors injustice and leans on love to rise above all the divisions and hate in the world. Moreover, to slow down in the Spirit and to hear the call of Breath, as Thompkins encourages us to do, is an act of self-love even before one attempts to love another person. Love yourself so you can love your neighbor as you work for justice and peace. Every week and every day are opportunities to abide in the love of God in order to love God, oneself, and others.

These devotions lead readers to love because Thompkins's words are linguistic icons to the love of God. This is the heart of doing justice and making peace in the world—love. And thankfully, this love won't let us go and it will be what will change us to become more like God, who is love, created us to be.

Read these pages and you'll hear the love song of the Spirit blowing. May that Holy Wind inspire you to sing a song full of faith, hope, and love, especially when the road isn't easy. But always remember, in order to sing with power and spiritual support, breathe, deeply, in and out, so that who you are on the inside matches what you do on the outside.

Rev. Dr. Luke A. Powery
Dean of Chapel
Duke University
Durham, NC

Introduction

THE purpose of this work is to offer an accessible spiritual tool for support to those who are engaged in the enterprise of working for justice and peace in the world. Such work is often taxing in many ways. Chief among them is spirituality.

The intense work of organizing, speaking, seeking funding, and administrating the people and systems that are necessary to make an impact can easily obscure the original passion and mission behind these activities. Concurrent with this danger of a loss of focus is the presence of pains, disappointments, and inevitable betrayals that can diminish one's capacity to experience or express joy.

Finally, while this work attempts to be spiritual and multi-faith, it is also a personal confession of my faith. I am a Christian who accepts Jesus as a welcoming and inclusive savior of love. I hope this too comes through.

This work is arranged in the following manner. At the beginning of each week, there is a call to worship. This is a traditional call to gather the community and participate in a ceremony of an exhale of gratitude for the past week and an inhale of the revelation of the Spirit for the week to come.

After each call to worship, there follow five devotionals that unpack the themes and issues that are in the call to worship. These devotions are intended to be brief but not short. That is to say that their purpose is a launching point for prayer or meditation. They are not intended to be an end in themselves.

The intention is that this practice of devotion can be achieved in twenty to twenty-five minutes a day. It is a tithe of time in a twenty-four-hour day to breathe, listen, and ponder anew what this day can be. It is an invitation to stop and take care of yourself and tend to your wounds before you arise and take care of others. It is a chance to remember and celebrate the love and passion that drew you to the work that you are doing.

*God breathes into every human being the
capacity to hope. It is the oxygen that supplies
the breath for those who fight for justice
and peace. Breathe deeply and faint not!*

FTJR

Breathe

Call to Worship

WEEK ONE

OH, God, you have created the world, and we have made it what it has become. So, we come to consult the creator of all things to help us with the mess we have made and the order of things yet to be created among us.

In our politics, let us find the plumb line of justice. In our families, give us the blueprint for forgiveness. Teach us to act out of kindness and vigorously pursue peace among us and between us!

Holy Spirit, let our worship equip us with the supernatural mental, psychological, and social tools needed to create anew what only we and God can do!

Come, let's worship with abandonment of tribe, color, and kind to become one in the Spirit and one in our faith!

What is not in your hands is not out of hand

*"Oh God, you have created the world, and we have made
it what it has become. So, we come to consult the creator
of all things to help us with the mess we have made and
the order of things yet to be created among us..."*

BREATHE, remember that this is your call but not your burden. The
world has been here for the duration of time. The fight between evil
and good predates your existence. You joined this battle because of an
irresistible call. It was a call to take responsibility, not ownership.

You are not solely responsible for the outcome of your efforts.
Both your failures and your successes are part of creating a new narrative for the world. Human activity has always been significant, but it
has not been totally determinant of its own future. Relax, you are only
one part of a magnificent partnership with a greater creator's purpose
in the world.

Accept your blindness so that your spirit can open the eyes of
your faith to believe beyond the proximal feelings and emotions of your

circumstances. Yes, people such as yourself created this mess. Indeed, you are capable of cleaning it up.

Today, ponder anew your commitment to your passion. But do not take it on as a burden. Decide today that you will fight for justice and remain at peace. You will be passionate about people, and yet you will not give their indifference or lack of commitment the power to discourage your efforts. What is not in your hands is not out of hand!

Integrity Matters

"In our politics let us find the plumb line of justice...."

NOTHING is more suffocating than having the air sucked out of a room by political considerations. You are told to temper your goals because they are unattainable and unachievable. Compromise is the adult and mature thing to do. In such moments of realism, right and wrong can become subservient to votes, coalitions, and what is politically feasible. These considerations are so constricting as to take away the breath of your full-throated advocacy.

Today, stop and recover your breath. Consider the cost of compromise and remember the purpose of your efforts. Compromise and coalitions must be built on more than political expediency.

There must be a plumb line, or what is built will be unstable. It will utterly fall to the winds and adversity of opponents and allies alike. A plumb line is what builders use to determine the strength and integrity of what they are building. You need a plumb line.

These are non-negotiable. This is what is absolutely necessary for your participation in whatever coalition or relationship to be truly effective. Discerning the plumb line gives one the freedom to discover great flexibility and creativity without sacrificing the very reason for your involvement.

If you find yourself in the middle of a structure or relationship that does not conform to your core values, it will cost you more to stay than to go.

You have permission to breathe in your witness and your hope and not sacrifice your breath to the atmosphere of political expediency. When you have lost your breath, you are dying, even when you look as if you are winning.

Remember your Family

*"In our families give us the blueprint for forgiveness.
Teach us to act out of kindness and vigorously
pursue peace among us and between us!"*

TO the world, you are a friend, and to your family, whether biological or chosen, you have become a stranger. Such is the plight of many people who are consumed by the passion of a mission. It takes effort and energy to love people. We all have a finite amount of energy. Because our supply does not equal the demand, we have to make choices. More to the point, if we do not choose, choices are made by those who claim our energy.

Fighting for people is draining. A family is draining. But it is not an equal demand. Making policies and creating changes are wholly selfish endeavors. They require every waking effort. But they do not return an equal amount of energy. Rather, the blueprint of social justice, ministry, or community work is consumption of a leader to advance a people. The only compensation is remembrance and maybe the satisfaction of advancing the struggle.

In fact, the more successful you become, the more isolated and alienated you can become. In a quest to feel connected and cared for, great leaders do dumb things. Leaders have engaged in sexual, monetary, and socially destructive activities just to replenish a personal sense of intimacy and caring. Their isolation mixed with pride in self-sufficiency has led to an awkward silence between them and their families.

The blueprint of families, when they are healthy, is mutual self-sacrifice. Healthy families have the commitment to forgive and accept us as we are. The less one is in the presence of one's family the easier it is to forget that they know you and love you. They committed to being there on good and bad days. They think of you as a mother, father, sister, brother, partner, and child without regard to your accomplishments.

So today, remember who your family is before you lose the memory and practice of who they are supposed to be. Stop and reconnect with the neglected one. This is the pattern of justice, not just right policy but right relationship. Breathe from your soul and reconnect to the purpose of community, relationship, and transcendent love.

Optimism, Hope, and Integrity

Week One – Day Four

"Holy Spirit let our worship equip us with supernatural mental, psychological, and social tools needed to create anew what only we and God can do!"

HOPE peeks out from behind our assumptions and lived experiences to remind us that our tomorrows do not have to be determined by our yesterdays. The truth of the matter is that evil, hatred, and love have an easier task than those of us who work for justice and peace in the world. They appeal to hatred, fear, and hurt. Evil bends a dark narrative around the light of any event until it seems sinister and conspiratorial. Evil sows' distrust. It is not tethered to reality and facts. All of this would be very discouraging but, that evil, most of the time, loses. Humanity finds a way to rise above itself.

Compromise and cooperation do eventually emerge from historical harms and social inequalities. Perseverance, consistency, and constant building of relationships, education, and mobilizing people do move people forward. Indeed, as has been quoted by many advocates of justice and peace, it is a well-worn axiom, "The arc of the moral universe is long, but it bends toward justice." *

This optimism and hope do not flow from news reports and a sane assessment of the struggle. Justice, love, and hope are not the creations of humanity. They are bigger than us. They are not internal forces. These are the winds that move our struggle and animate our commitment.

When you become frustrated and fixated on the narrative of the success of evil, pause and consider the impossibility of love, the stubbornness of hope, and the power of faith. Ponder anew your experiences with these forces. Feel the strength flowing from their presence in our lives. Don't be afraid of being inexplicably optimistic about the task before you. Rely on a power greater than yourself that you cannot control and do not necessarily understand. The power of our humanity lies in our ability to not only think but also believe. Raise the sails of our thoughts and emotions and draw upon the resources of empathy, faith, and spirituality to feel the winds of change that are independent of our actions or intentions.

* see: https://quoteinvestigator.com/2012/11/15/arc-of-universe/

No lone rangers

*"Come let's worship with abandonment of tribe, color and
kind to become one in the Spirit and one in our faith!"*

IF we do not see our differences, we will not change. If we see only our
differences, we will not be able to change. Denying or ignoring the com-
position of those with whom we work is a certain key to ineffectiveness
and historical redundancy. Nevertheless, it is not easy to accomplish
our goal of diversity and, certainly, inclusion.

This is not because it is not natural. Biologically, we are adaptive
and inquisitive creatures. We were born with an innate curiosity to be
fascinated by and engage in things like us and unlike us. But, alas, we
were socialized to suppress our urges to plunge into diversity. Even those
of us who value it can, without warning, find ourselves in exclusive
enclaves, cocooned in a thick barrier of rational justifications for why
it is so hard to bring diversity or inclusion into the struggle for justice
and peace.

No one is immune to social inertia. After all, there is so much less
challenge there. It is fun. It is familiar. It is affirming. But to be clear, the
exclusion does not come without a whole lot of effort, both on our part

and that of those who came before us. Religious, economic, gender, racial, and sexual homogeneity always involve erasure, ignoring, and exclusion. Diversity is the natural state of things. Historically, exclusivity has been a constructed and intentional reality. Even if we want to change the story, we must first acknowledge that we started in the middle of others' stories. And, without a great deal of effort, their practices and outcomes will be our stories.

No one has clean hands or histories on this exclusion. Yes, there are real power dynamics within real groups that make us unequal. But all of us, regardless of status and characteristics, are awash in the currents and eddies of our communities' exclusionary and exclusive activities.

We experience guilt, frustration, and then resignation about the lack of diversity in our social circle or workspace. But ultimately, this resignation is not an option. The answers and solutions to our struggle for justice and peace can only come when we ask the right questions. Until everyone is in the room with a voice, the questions are not there. Therefore, the strategies, emotional breakthroughs, and revelations will never happen.

Breathe. Overcome the inertia of acceptance of the way things are. Deny the justification of geography, race, class, sexual orientation, or religious affiliation and open your eyes. Open your spirit to see all the colors of the rainbow and decide that monochrome relationships and communities are not acceptable. Eschew the inward navel gazing meditation of simple personal enlighten.

The answers are not discoverable by a lone ranger on a quest for enlightenment. They are found in the questions and challenges of others that call from the depths of our souls the wisdom and folly of our humanity.

Dance, laugh, and love others who are different by letting yourself believe that these are sacred acts of engagement. They are not distractions from the mission. Believe that, without the other, our fight is futile. Talk, play, compromise, and collaborate; these are essential functions for humanity to live together and find ways to show mercy and be at peace with one another.

Let's Keep Practicing Love
Until We Get It Right!

FTJR

Recover

Call to Worship

WEEK TWO

GOD, *we worship in hope, and we praise in faith. We run to your presence because we need your perspective. The tragedies are too close to our sight, so they have blurred our vision. Today, restore our vision. Let us encounter anew what you can do.*

Where violence and pain seem ubiquitous, guide us to that place and space in our hearts and the world that is filled with hope and healing. Where social ideologies of racial, religious, and sectarian prejudice flood our media and the conversations around us turn up the volume on the Good a News of the Gospel.

In our worship, we need an encounter with the divine. We will not stop at hearsay or second-hand experience. We need a personal audience with the sovereign of the universe. We need to feel the matriarchal compassion and strength of God and the patriarchal assertion of the power and control of God! We want to see the suffering servant and the risen Lord. We need to see Jesus. Give us more than inspiration. Give us an importation from heaven! Come, with desperation and hope—let's worship the God of our restoration and redemption.

Turn toward the Light

*"The tragedies are too close to our sight so that they
have blurred our vision. Today restore our vision.
Let us encounter anew what you can do...."*

LIVES are at stake. Death, pain, and suffering are the consequences of injustice and violent conflict. Daily, our lives are filled with the struggle for policies, relationships, equality, and inclusion. But, every once in a while, we are faced with the reality that we are really fighting against the destruction of human lives.

It is at funerals and in prisons, crying with victims and shaking our heads over the destruction of natural resources that we will never get back, that we see preventable tragedies. We experience profound grief. Grief can debilitate or even destroy our ability to move forward.

Everyone who fights for justice and peace struggles with the shockwaves of pain that come from being witnesses to these things. Our proximity to the stories and realities of the failure of human kindness can pull us into a vortex of anger, despair, and cynicism. In these instances, we want to self-medicate, escape, engage in self-destructive activity, or just run away for a while and cry. At these times, such action seems as effective as any other course of action that we have tried.

But before giving into such moroseness, stop! Look again at the faces of those who have been touched by human indifference and cruelty. While you were looking at them, they were looking at you.

You cannot see your own light or the importance of that light to someone in darkness. Your efforts, though small and seemingly insignificant, are efforts that provide the sparks of hope that people need to get through their darkest nights.

Yes, you lost, and the consequences of that loss are devastating. However, your struggle itself is a win. Don't underestimate the power of the inspiration of your battle to both heal the wounded and call to arms new soldiers. Remember, your vision was not simply to change the world but to change those of us in the world.

Stop, open your eyes, and behold the life around you and the possibilities that are still before you.

Recover from the Lies

Week Two – Day Two

"Where social ideologies of racial, religious, and sectarian prejudices flood our media and the conversations around us, Oh God turn up the volume on the Good a News of the Gospel..."

EVIL is loud. It is boastful. It is bombastic. Evil does not speak. It shouts! We are surrounded by people who are self-promoting ideologues. They play for the crowd. They garner likes on Facebook, Instagram, and Twitter. They build brands and promote a perception of popularity and success.

We know that their influence will be short-lived, and their success is a mile wide and an inch deep. Nonetheless, we are discouraged by their existence and the enthusiasm with which bigotry, xenophobia, violence, and pride are being celebrated. Like the powerful winds formed in a firestorm, these self-indulgent claims can suck the optimism out of our outlook and suffocate our hope. They can cause the breath of our faith to become labored.

They are liars. Lies need believers. Lies need the silence of the truth. Lying is the art of deceiving until lies replace facts as the basis of reality. So, the loss of breath and then our voice is particularly insidious.

These lies can and do illicit a nagging envy. Popularity, after all, brings with it the power to influence. We suppose that if we had the power of their popularity, we would be able to save lives.

Therein lies the fallacy of this avalanche of feelings and justification for discouragement. The truth has never had a crowd. Love has always been ridiculed and disrespected. Popularity has always been illusive for the truly brave. Yet humanity has seemingly avoided self-destruction. It has always been saved by the dogged perseverance of those who would not accept defeat.

The good news is that human beings have been created with the capacity to think, feel, and believe. Empathy, though it can be suppressed for a season, has never been able to be obliterated.

It is the witness of the Christian gospel and many other religious traditions that in embracing weakness, there is a strength of a type that overcomes evil. In the act of believing, there is an intention of hope and consciousness that collectively forms a sphere of influence that permeates the hearts of even the most callous. By courageously speaking the truth, taking on the pain of others, and demonstrating love, circumstances change.

Place yourself in a silent room and listen to your heartbeat. Remember that this rhythmic sound of a muscle is the beat of the miraculous power of faith, pulsating with hope, replenishing energy, and brimming with imagination for the next generation. Listen closely to this persistent, small, and continuous sound of life, praying that you and I do not quit.

Recover from Toxic Faith

"We will not stop at a hearsay or second-hand experience. We need a personal audience with the sovereign of the universe. We need to feel the matriarchal compassion, the strength of God and the patriarchal assertion of the power and control of God."

IT is an astonishing and undeniable fact that the human capacity to have faith can become its most destructive or its most generative characteristic. The notion of God, the idea of spirituality, and the belief in a deity of some kind are frightening because they are so powerful.

In fact, faith, religion, and spirituality are both toxic and cleansing. In their most toxic forms, they are nothing other than a projection of power and pettiness for control. Or, equally as odorous, they are self-indulgent navel-gazing that eschews the issues of power and the relevance of human complicity in the world. In this instance, enlightenment then becomes another powerful way to ignore or justify injustice and accept unresolved historical harms.

So, those who are in the struggle for justice and peace have sometimes been embarrassed by the fact that many of us are motivated and called to this work because of our faith. When we are described as faithful or spiritual people, we hasten to say that we do not mean to be such things. This act of differentiation can so occupy our time and energy that we lose the value and power of being faithful, religious, or spiritual.

Let go of the burden of having to explain your faith. After all, you are not trying to impose it on others or deny it to anyone. Don't accept the invitations from those who want to argue about the experience of the world and not understand the motivating and powerful experience of your faith. You are not responsible for explaining anything about another's faith. You are only privilege to live out loud the motivation and power of your faith.

We access our inspiration from different experiences with one another and the divine. We do not have to rely on second-hand experiences. We can note, learn from, and reject the experiences of others who use faith to be destructive and yet celebrate who we are in order to do what we must do.

We can be critical of the effects of toxic realities while imbibing the aroma of the life-giving narratives and experiences that we have in our lives. Injustice and violence in the name of a faith or religion that are as disturbing as are such things done in the name of people who deny the experience or existence of God. Both should be confronted and called for what they are. The work that you do in religious spaces is the as sacred work that you do in so-called secular spaces. Wherever we are loving and living, it is sacred.

So, let go of the special "burden" of your faith. You neither need to apologize, deny, or support injustice or violence from people who share your designation because they do not share your faith. Lay hold of the unique power of your belief to motivate, critique, and call you to change and challenge the world.

Recover from "Jesus"

Week Two – Day Four

"We want to see the suffering servant and the risen Lord. We need to see Jesus..."

SO much of western society's understanding of itself is predicated upon the mythology of Jesus. Its ethics, morality, and sense of righteousness are measured by our supposed fidelity to Jesus. Churches the size of football and soccer stadiums gather on a weekly basis to experience the corporate celebration of the life and words of Jesus.

So, the narrative of what Jesus would have done is important, whether you and I are Christians or not. For some people of faith, Jesus' death is an inspiration for continuing revelation. It is not limited to a historical phenomenon. Rather, Jesus is the progenitor of a new movement of compassion, grace, and justice.

For others, Jesus is a standard of social and cultural marker that must be defended. Jesus is in fact wedded to the notion of certain moral and social norms. Thus, rendering to these norms of behavior a religious fever. In either case, Jesus can be a reason for peace or a reason for war. He can be a liberating force for freedom or a justifying argument for injustice.

It is therefore more than a religious matter to discern a clear image of Jesus. It may be a personal decision to ignore or deny the significance of Jesus, but it is not possible to do so on a global or societal basis. One's encounter and description of Jesus is an unavoidable task of fighting for peace of justice.

The question, of course, is not about Jesus. It is about his actions and significance. Stop and consider the message or possible implementation of the way in which Jesus lived and reportedly died. Consider the way in which Jesus is regarded by others. Even if you do not agree with someone's interpretation of Jesus, or even if you strongly disagree with their understanding of Jesus, you must find a way to respect their faith as the motivating factor for their actions. This one action alone, truly respecting the faith and beliefs of another, will allow us to engage with someone with authenticity and impact. People are not only biology they are belief and traditions.

The most difficult thing that we may ever do is have empathy for someone whose pain is neither real for us nor important for us. Empathy is not to be practiced with discrimination. Empathy is a tool for justice and peace. We can either consider people as enemies or as people with whom we can and must create transforming friendships.

Recover the Sound of the Call

Week Two – Day Five

*"Give us more than inspiration. Give us an importation
from heaven! Come, with a desperation and a hope..."*

UTOPIA will always be no place until someone has the stubborn insistence that it is real. Don't be apologetic about being a dreamer. Don't allow people to dismiss your lofty vision of what humanity can and will be by insisting that it is an unattainable fantasy.

In every spiritual vision and religious system, there is an inspirational ideal that not only gives us goals but also imparts energy and strength for the attainment of the impossible. This is the essence of a political goal, a moral desire, or a spiritual longing. It is for a place that calls us, not just a process that preoccupies us.

Aristotle writes, "Some ultimate end, final goal must exist which we want for its sake, and not simply as a means to something else. There must be and end in itself: and this is logically necessary, otherwise we have simply an infinite regress. You cannot value everything as a means to an end, unless something is the end, the ultimate value." *

Don't apologize for the sense of call and passion. This is a great generative engine of ideas that helps us discover resources that we did not know we had. It changes our approach to the problems. We are not wondering if it is possible. We are simply discovering how to bring it to past. Consequently, this ideal helps us create new pathways and means to get to our destination. We are responding, not just instigating. Something greater than ourselves must insist that it is possible. Until the consciousness of many become change their will not be the change in any.

Martin Luther King's dream. Plato's ideal, the Buddha's dharma, and Jarena Lee's epochal call to ministry are examples of people who did forthrightly claim that their vision was not of their making but of their response to something greater than themselves.

Stop and tend to the wounds of those who have called you foolish. Listen again to the small voice calling you to address that which is impossible. Embrace again a dream that you thought was a fantasy. Breathe deeply and commit to the dream; walk the way of the calling. Utopia, heaven, and hope are desperately calling. Let those who have ears hear and declare it shall be!

*https://campus.aynrand.org/campus/globals/transcripts/ aristotles-ethics-and-politics-happiness-reason-and-the-ideal-society

When we swat at flies we often miss, hit ourselves, and become more distracted by our actions than the nonbiting insect could have ever done. Flies have a short lifetime of irritation, and your life has long-term historical significance!

FTJR

Relationships

Call to Worship

WEEK THREE

WITH profound exhaustion, we gather to worship you. We are drowning in a world of contention and strife. Some of it, because of its importance, is worthy of our attention. Some of it is a distraction from our peace.

Let our worship restore our balance and give us the gift of discernment to see what is important and dismiss what is extraneous. Fill us with a deep well of tranquility that cannot be emptied by all that seeks to drain us of our energy and hope.

May our worship unite us in purpose to lift up the name, message, and person of Jesus. The Holy Spirit moves us beyond our allegiance to tribe, nation, and culture to a commitment to seek dignity and justice for all human beings. Remind us that we are your ambassadors of love, not warriors of anger and division.

Come, let us drink from the fountain of worship and be washed, replenished, and filled again.

Weaponized faith and monetized information

Week Three – Day One

> *"With profound exhaustion we gather to worship you.*
> *We are drowning in a world of contention and strife.*
> *Some of it, because of its importance, is worthy of our*
> *attention. Some of it is but a distraction to our peace."*

IT is a simple truth that, if we want to be different, we must be different. We have to have the humility to understand that our voice is unique but not singular. To be a person of faith is to believe that the breath and voice of the Spirit do not only reside in our bodies. Realize that winning arguments is not the only way the spirit moves.

Those who are committed to change and progress are in constant contact with people who persistently declare the impending destruction of the world and the doom of human existence. At the center of their passion is a heartbeat of concern. For the most part, this concern creates the force of a movement. It is the energy of volunteerism and even self-sacrifice. It is a good thing to study the problems that one is addressing. Research, investigative reporting, and following developments on social media are useful activities for the concerned and caring. However, these very activities can fuel a raging fire of debilitating anxiety.

This is all the truer because many of the people who are bellowing their opinions and influencing their followers employ cynical methods of manipulation of people, information, and emotions. The business model of social media companies is based on monetizing reactions and conflict. This has led to a torrent of misinformation and the worse forms of grandstanding and gaslighting. Even the "traditional" new sources have assumed dramatic editorial lenses to communicate otherwise straightforward facts.

Weaponized and monetized information creates a powerful magnet that intentionally and unintentionally sucks people into wells of vitriol, angry argumentation, and the venoms of cynicism and despair. Or, as the old African American phrase puts it, "it puts us on the thin side of evil, trying not to break through."

There is a thin line between advocacy and fanaticism, passion and obsession, and discussion and argumentation. It is all too easy to be pulled across the line. We must be mindful to engage in our advocacy with the intention not to fall into the wells or slide over the aforementioned lines. Our methods, tones, and words cannot simply be reactionary. It must always be in the service of not just the argument but the relationship.

Trolling is not prophetic. Being snide, crass, or sarcastic will gain likes, but it will not help us be heard. When we cannot find it within ourselves to answer in a way that will not diminish our own spirit or debase our sense of kindness, our faith is tested. Do not react. Stop before you hit send, write the email, or yell at the person in front of you.

Consider if and how you can comment or engage without doing harm to yourself or another person.

It is a great act of trust and faith to let the spirit speak. It is an act of civil and spiritual disruption to resist the myth of the absolute power of social media and disinformation and simply not give it a reaction. It is sometimes an act of self-care, prophetic resistance, and effective witness to ignore the baseless and senseless thing that you cannot address without doing harm to yourself or your witness. It does not mean that the Spirit will not speak. It just means that the voice of justice is a chorus, not a solo.

Doing is not Being

*"Fill us with a deep well of tranquility that cannot be emptied
by all that seeks to drain us of our energy and hope."*

EMBEDDED in the term *activism* is the notion of movement and bustle. Apart from the outcomes themselves, activists, organizers, ministers, and do-gooders measure their success by the volume of activities in which they are involved. Appointments, marches, phone calls, the scheduling of events, and meetings with friends and foes alike give us the quantitative and emotional volume that contributes to our sense of progress. Overall, one thing that can be said of ourselves is that we are doers; doing becomes our being.

Inasmuch as it is effective, doing, becomes a high. It also becomes the way others see us. We become the "go-to people" to "get something done." The more successful we are, the greater our investment in our identity as a doer. But this is not without significant downsides that become more evident the longer one dedicates oneself to doing it.

Doing has the price of draining our energy and exposing us in equal measure to success and frustration. Being the doer and the catalyst to get others to do also exposes one to the isolation of being an inspiration, a hero, and a person unlike those who are being led. Even Jesus could not convince his disciples that he needed them (Gethsemane). One does not have to be arrogant or self-promoting to be trapped in the cage of loneliness and isolation.

Although doing is the psychological drug of our choice and the currency for purchasing our sense of success, we must accept the idea that it has three unhealthy side effects: 1) it creates a codependent relationship with those with whom we work by convincing them that their failures of commitment will be covered by our ability to overcommit; 2) it diminishes our need for and therefore practice of faith in something or someone greater than ourselves and our efforts; and 3) it drains one of the energies to celebrate the victories because the work of the constant struggle blocks out the success of the moment.

Create your own island of tranquility in your sea of appointments, meetings, and stressful interactions. Practice letting go. That, too, is a skill. Do something for yourself that no one asked you to do. Walk, run, journal, or simply sit and think about all the wonders in the world. Practice saying "no" without explanation or excuse. Say to yourself. . . my being is not doing. . . my being is simply to be my best me. . .

Communities and Rallies

Week Three – Day Three

*"May our worship unite us in purpose to lift up
the name, message, and person of Jesus."*

IT is curious to see how faith can unite people in such divisive and destructive ways and yet claim to have kind intentions. In fact, faith and religion have amazing effects of strength, personal insight, and powerful experiences of indwelling of what only be described as a mystical impartation of strength and an inexhaustible hope. This is particularly true in the experience of communal worship.

There is something so amazing about being in the presence of a community that is focused on accessing a part of the human experience and connecting with the ineffable presence of the divine. Whether through singing, dancing, chanting, the telling of the myths of victories over the struggle of annihilation, or through other means of expressing a communal longing and expressive joy, worship is a heady experience. However, worship, as with faith and religion itself, can become a rally of self-projection, arrogant assumptions about the world, and a terrifying group think of judgment and anger.

Something can go terribly wrong. One can find oneself in the middle of people who profess and indeed practice individual kindness, yet project and practice communal exclusion and bullying. It can diminish our capacity to love instead of expanding our responsibility to care. One can find oneself in the dysphoric state of being in a place of comfort and confusion. The community that is central to one's identity and understanding of the inevitability of good conquering evil can itself adopt practices, say words, and use images that perpetuate harm and destruction in the world around them.

The faith community can create its own self-aware ego (label, brand, and hierarchal structure) and adopt an agenda of self-preservation. It replaces the fragile and humble experience of seeking the divine with the notion that it is, itself, divinely inspired. As always, when human ego supplants faithful longing for religion and faith becomes a justification for acts of hubris and declarations of power, then it becomes an agent of control intent imposing on others the community's standards and ways of acting and believing. Or, in other words, it becomes the very thing that caused the faithful to seek the divine.

While this can indeed happen in any faith tradition, for those of us who find our identity in the actions of Jesus, this is particularly heartbreaking. Many of the actions of Jesus were to overturn the boundaries of identity, class, and gender with the force of love, grace, and justice. Many of the people who worship with us have stories of life-changing experiences with Jesus, as do those who faithfully believe that God is intimately interested in our well-being in the world. Yet, when we gather, we do not uplift the spirit nor affirm the earth-shattering revelation and life enhancing loving and living God of liberation.

Seeking God can be a communal activity. But finding God is always an individual discovery. The church, synagogue, temple, mosque, or other places where one seeks God in community are all witnesses to faithful traditions whose intended function is to focus your journey, but it is not their mission to constrain it. The way we love our community is to raise our voices and practice our faith in our communities, even when it is uncomfortable. You are not being disloyal when you are faithful to your own spiritual journey. Challenging the status quo because of your revelation of spirit, when it differs from those around you, is not an act of disloyalty. Let go of the naïve spiritual expectation of complete agreement with your worshipping community. Remember your quest and embrace the journey.

What others do not understand is that the within the tension and the contention of community is in fact a part of that which endears us to community. Faith in the challenge of community creates the strength of our convictions. Our hurts and our celebrations save us from the selfishness of an individualized spirituality of convenience.

Friends, Allies
and Siblings

*Holy Spirit move us beyond our allegiance to tribe,
nation, and culture to a commitment to seek the
dignity and justice for all human beings.*

IT is difficult to disagree with people without defining them as enemies
and those who stand with us as friends. "Us and them" are the universal
terms of conflict. Even with the purest of intentions, this vilification of
others seems inevitable. This is even more probable when our conflict
is about the safety of others, the survival of the planet, or the dignity
of our friends.

If we are not careful, our struggle to do good and change the world
can infect us with anger, revenge, and sarcasm. We can find ourselves
entertaining fantasies of violence against our opponents. We secretly
celebrate others' demise and embarrassment. Because this was never our
intention, we can be in deep personal denial of our own state of hurt and
anger. We want to regard ourselves as the good ones. We define ourselves

by who we are not. After all, one of the principal characteristics of an enemy is that they are not like us.

Further, we reduce our definition of friends to the singular function of ally. An ally agrees with us. Fights for the issues that are important to us. Our friendships, indeed, every relationship in our lives, can become constricted by our social and political battles. We can find ourselves constantly in conflict with those whom we love as well as with any new person that we meet who does not immediately share our social, political, or spiritual views. Quite unintentionally we can fall prey to the adage "we have met the enemy and the enemy is us."

If you are not careful, you can become a caricature of an angry person who has only grace for those who are like us. This is the inevitable effect of defining our human siblings merely as enemies and insisting that our friends be purely aligned with our beliefs and practices. The problem with this world of enemies and allies is that there is no process of redemption. Identity and affinity are a thin linguistic veneer covering up prejudice and intolerance.

It is both spiritually and physically challenging to remember that we are siblings. Stop and breathe. Remember and honor your own journey to your passions and enlightenment by recalling the grace that others gave you. Calling people to account is not to discount or excuse their participation in the hurtful systems, nor is it to avoid naming their personally hurtful actions.

Rather, the intent of the work of justice and peace is to create a safe place to work with those with whom we must live, love, and work together for the betterment of one another and the planet on which we live. People are in our way of achieving our goals. Loving, forgiving, and engaging with people is the path to all our success.

Superheroes are cartoons

Week Three – Day Five

*"Come let us drink from the fountain of worship
and be washed, replenished, and filled again."*

WE come to this work out of passion. We, like Moses in the Hebrew Scriptures, have stories of being called into the commitment of attempting the daring enterprise of caring and working for change because of the burning bush. Some of us come slowly, through a process of education and experience. Some of us were moved by a singular event or tragedy. In these instances, it is our passion that guides us and creates the energy of our work in the world.

However, when it is reactive, passion is also dangerous. It can literally consume our lives in spectacular flames of protest and anger. Moses' bush burned, but it did not consume him. It garnered the attention of the prophet, but it was not destructive to either the prophet or the world around him. Precisely because it was light without heat and effective without being destructive, that is what made it a spiritual metaphor.

Far too often the stories of our heroes are ones of self-sacrifice and of mavericks who will do what has to be done to get things done. These are people who wrote powerful words and moved people to achieve amazing changes, yet their bodies were broken. They suffered financial ruin. Their human relationships were characterized by respect but not love. Simply put, their passion consumed them. We then erect monuments of academic study, mythical stories, and sometimes actual statues to these people. Implicitly and sometimes unconsciously, we internalize the idea that this is the pattern of success in social justice. Sadly, the martyr is the message.

It is a strange irony that the entire reason for the work we do is to lessen suffering in the world. Yet we have accepted that suffering and loss are the pathways to effecting change in the world. It is especially ironic for Christians, who are always talking about the "scandal of the cross." It is as if some have conflated our identity with that of Jesus—that is the ultimate sacrilege. This is the reason that we abuse the time, talent, and emotions of the leaders of the movement for justice in the world. Underpaying, overworking, and dismissing the cost of the stress and exhaustion of continuously being called upon to always lead and always give of yourself is accepted as normal.

Suffering is not a requirement for effectiveness. You do not have to lose your life so that others can gain theirs. You don't have to feel guilty for being paid, taking a vacation, or not speaking out on every issue. You can save yourself while saving the world. In fact, it is not your job to save the world. It is your job to live your best life and help others live theirs.

It is an act of hubris and faithlessness to accept the idea that you must deny your personal joy in order to be taken seriously in the struggle for justice and peace in the world. Reject internally and externally the idea that your life is the reservoir of others' refreshment. You are not being selfish by caring about yourself. Remember that you too are part of the world that you are called to care for.

Some days you must remind yourself:
"I've had better days and I will have better days.
Today is the anomaly. It is not the pattern."

FTJR

Feelings

WEEK FOUR

THROWING *off our masks of civility, we come open and honest to worship our God. We admit that we are angry and disappointed. We are struggling with loving one another and caring about those who clearly do not care about us.*

Let your loving and powerful presence surround us with the light of grace.

Show us a way to forgive without a sense of loss.

We bring our tears for the harmed and the hurting.

Lead us to a pathway to kindness that does not feel as though it is weakness.

We are tired of the shaming and blaming, the bullying, and the gaslighting.

We need an adjustment in our spirit to reclaim the joy of God and the peace that comes from the knowledge of God's faithfulness.

Come, Holy Spirit, and save us from the temptation of our pride and ego to see ourselves as purely right and others as always wrong.

We welcome your correction and your challenge through scripture and the testimonies of others. Give us a worship that changes us and creates a new heart and a right spirit.

Show up, Holy God, and bring the refining fire. Convert the heat of our anger into a furnace of holy activity without destructive intentions or outcomes. We cannot do this on our own.

We desperately worship to be reminded that we do not and cannot do this on our own. So, come all who are ready to be honest and encounter the truth of who God is, who we are, face the truth of what we could have done, should have done and yet still must do. Let us worship God Almighty!

Anger Ain't all bad

Week Four – Day One

*"We admit that we are angry and disappointed. We
are struggling with loving one another and caring
about those who clearly do not care about us."*

ANGER, hurt, and outrage are strong feelings. Sometimes, they are also appropriate feelings. It is particularly harmful and disingenuous to say that those who fight for justice and contend for peace must be tranquil and stoic. Nothing could be further from the truth. To be in the struggle to change things is to be surrounded by conflict and contention. Perhaps what is most jarring about our anger is that it is a shared emotion with those with whom we are in conflict. Emotional harm is a part of conflict. Anger is part of the reason for change. It is a part of the process of change. It sometimes results from the outcome of change. It is inevitable.

Detachment is an ineffective and personally harmful plan. People will attempt to make you deny your own anger in service to the myth that anger is a sign of immaturity. What others cannot do is stop you from being angry. They can only get you to try to repress your anger. It is a well-known medical fact that repressed anger contributes to mental health symptoms related to anxiety and depression.* In fact, it is too much to ask to look upon the harm of conversion therapy, police brutality, planetary destruction, ethnic cleansing, and the pitting of people against one another for the promotion of a few people and not in fact be angry.

We should not deny ourselves the dignity of anger. We have the right to be outraged. It is personally harmful to suppress or repress your anger. The image of outraged protestors and yelling detractors will also be used to diminish the legitimacy of the victims' cries. Pejorative descriptions of this anger (mad, unhinged, etc.) are hurled at you, hoping to strike down the potency of your passion. It is not immature to be angry. The measure of maturity and effectiveness is what one does with anger.

Unmanaged anger can also be particularly dangerous to communication and coalition building. It can become mistrust, which is the anticipation of harm. Our optimism can morph into the poison of pessimism. Unmanaged anger will magnify the points of disagreement and diminish our markers of progress. It will turn up the volume of offense. Unmanaged anger changes the tone of our work and our engagement with friends and foes alike.

We are not responsible for others' anger. However, no one is responsible for lessening or addressing our own anger. Anger is not dissipated by an apology or even by change. It is a personal choice to let it go. You must decide that anger is not working for you. Don't be ashamed or dismissive of your anger. Admit it. Embrace it. It is not a spiritual discipline to ignore your anger. It is a sign of spiritual exercise to deal redemptively with your anger. Ask yourself: Is this anger hurting me or helping me? Is this anger affecting your sleep or peace?

The root causes of anger are fear, lack of control, and unrecognized harm. Recognize that nothing you can do will lessen these causes. They are constant. You are not in control of these things. Your only issue is to decide to who or what do you trust is in control. Remember, the God who called you is also able to protect you and provide for the redress of unjust treatment. Working through anger is an opportunity to reaffirm and strengthen our practical faith. You don't have to let go, but you must surrender.

* https://thriveworks.com/anger-management-counseling/

Forgiveness Not
A Requirement

"Show us a way to forgive without a sense of loss."

FORGIVENESS is a noble thing. But it is a hard thing. It's only relevant when hurt, harm, and pain are linked with culpability and guilt. It exists as an alternative to the more understandable options of revenge and annihilation of the people who are responsible for the harm. Forgiveness is counterintuitive to self-protection.

Forgiveness seems fundamentally unfair. It is unsatisfying. Therefore, it is always an intentional and unmerited act of great mental, spiritual, and psychological effort. Forgiveness should not be regarded as an automatic or obligated response. Anyone who struggles to offer others forgiveness should not be regarded as spiritually deficient. It is not an easy thing. The question is: Is it the best thing?

Worse yet, forgiveness can be weaponized. It can be employed as a cynical part of a strategy of avoidance of consequences. Confession with a request for forgiveness is an incantation with the expectation of the suspension of moral, political, and sometimes criminal consequences.

Such an apology with a request for forgiveness is a way of calling into question the authenticity of the faith of their victims and those who stand with them. This is especially true for those who are part of religious or spiritual communities.

These communities are defined by their assertion of the power and importance of forgiveness. We celebrate mercy. We have forged a notion of grace based on our scriptural and sacred texts. We are the ones who assert that, after the truth is told, we must forgive. Indeed, history has taught us that the cycle of revenge is never-ending. So, every society that wants to break the cycle of war must find the courage to engage in ceremonies and policies that offer public forgiveness, after accountability.

That having been said, forgiveness is the goal. But the process is not linear and has to negotiate the eddies and currents of pain and hurt. No one must forgive. If, and when, we do forgive, it does not have the expectation of lessening or deleting the consequences. Forgiveness is a personal choice for healing. As a choice, it is a process of thought, prayer, and personal exploration about the consequences it has upon oneself. You do not have to forgive in a hurry. After a massacre, in the wake of an atrocity, or in the ashes of shattered lives, demanding forgiveness is a burden too heavy to bear.

Take as much time as you need. In this instance, a delay will not lead to a denial. No one who has harmed another has the right to expect forgiveness. You, however, have the privilege of considering whether you want to forgive them for your own healing or health. Relax, your decision will not mean that their actions are any less reprehensible or culpable. While it may be true that forgiveness is a definite part of the path to peace and justice, they do not have to occur at the same time or at the same pace.

Kindness is a weapon

Week Four – Day Three

*"Lead us to a pathway to kindness that does
not feel as though it is weakness."*

WHAT is so suspicious about being kind? Why is kindness often viewed as a sign of weakness? What is weak about being regarded as friendly, generous, and considerate? Why are kind people labeled as naïve? Why is the goal of kindness often seen as opposed to the struggle for justice? These, of course, are false assumptions and assertions. The truth is you do not have to be choose between being kind or affective.

You have the right to be yourself. Kindness is a means by which we attempt to assert our optimism about change and people. Being kind is a way that we use our personal power to create emotional space for changes in people. The more that kindness is unexpected, the more effective it is. Kindness is a militant expression of empathy and an expectation that human beings will choose to do good. What makes this all the more powerful is that kindness is not reactionary. It is proactive. Therefore, it is both courageous and prophetic. Kindness extends grace to people who have not earned it. The more one understands injustice, the greater the emotional and spiritual strength for those who choose to be strong enough to be kind, knowing that there is a great possibility that it may not be returned.

So, it is a curious and hurtful thing to be ridiculed and dismissed for being kind. This, not just from those who oppose us but from our allies. Our friends and allies often see kindness as a soft response to a hard reality. To be clear, it is not the kindness that is offered to them. It is the kindness shown to those whom we mutually see as obstacles to peace and justice. Or it is not a problem when kindness is not authentic but rather a form of manipulation by showing false interest in our opponents.

What your friends and foes alike don't understand is that your commitment to kindness is a means by which you guard your heart against fossilization. In the struggle for justice, one can become hardened against mercy and dismissive of the very idea of redemption. Without a personal commitment to and practice of regarding human beings as siblings, we will inevitably lose our ability to recognize and encourage the powerful human traits of empathy, compassion, and self-sacrifice.

Your kindness is a superpower of love. It is an aggressive recruitment tool for change. Authentically and doggedly continue to exercise of your muscle of expectation about people being better. Persistent kindness is a subversive and powerful force in recruiting allies of love and justice in the world.

It's alright to be not alright

*"We need an adjustment in our spirit to reclaim
the joy of God and the peace that comes from
the knowledge of God's faithfulness."*

A mixture of exhaustion, anger, and frustration can drain the hope and optimism from your vision and expectations. These can cause your soul to ask the questions of relevancy and resiliency. "What is it all for?" Does it matter?" "Do things really change when they change?" "Why are lies so well compensated and the truth tellers are so undervalued." Progress occurs at a glacial pace. Every step forward is greeted with people who pledge to fight for regression.

Nothing has changed in the work. It just feels different. These questions of effectiveness are always swirling around us, but, depending on one's mental state, social engagement, and financial means, our reaction to these questions changes.

The problem is not the questions or the answers. We must be careful to not trivialize our personal struggle with faith. Our external battle for justice and peace in the world is an extension of an internal quest for making meaning in the world for ourselves. Our experience with the divine or feelings about God will inevitably wax and wane with our circumstances, disappointments, and challenges. Pay attention to these feelings. Left unattended, they can lead to a loss of oneself as one tries to save the world.

Admit your doubts, feelings of inadequacy, and fears. Don't fold into the silence of isolation. The physical and mental effects of living in the tension of change and advocacy are too heavy a burden to carry alone. By the mere fact that you care about injustice you have chosen to shoulder the weight of others hurts and pains.

Create an intentional plan and strategy for your physical and mental health. Plan for disappointments, guard against exhaustion, and create a space and time in your life to step away from the trauma and drama of the struggle to change the world. Give yourself the time and space to reconnect with the mystery and majesty of your faith. Be selfish about your own mental and physical health. One of the greatest acts of faith is believing that loving ourselves is part of the change that we are fighting for on behalf of others. If you do not have a strategy for self-care, your idea of kindness, empathy, and grace is inadequate to bring about justice in the world.

Pray and meditate, but also talk to others about your feelings. Seek professional counseling. Enjoy fun activities without guilt; play. Allow yourself to pursue pleasurable experiences without dread that they will diminish your focus. Abandon yourself in worship and wonder of the natural and supernatural. Laugh with gusto without fear of being called silly. While you are fighting for the lives of others, remember to live your life. Living is loving, and joy is the not-so-secret weapon of the struggle for justice. It turns struggle into dancing and fighting into singing. Dance! Sing! Live!

The owner of Vulnerability

"Come, Holy Spirit, and save us from the
temptation of our pride and ego to see ourselves as
purely right and others as always wrong."

PEOPLE who do not believe that they can make a difference usually do not. Working for change requires an enormous amount of confidence. At a minimum, it presumes at least two things. 1) that we know what is wrong; and 2) that we believe that our actions can be a part of fixing it. When you are trying to change and/or challenge things, humility, timidity, and subtlety are not rewarded. Rather, boldness, risk taking, and a good deal of stubbornness are expected and celebrated.

Our struggle leaves us little room for self-reflection. Flexibility is viewed with suspicion. Unexamined arrogance is a dangerous byproduct of our work and passion. Without realizing it, we can become as ridged and doctrinaire as those with whom we contend. Our moral certainty can morph into an immoral prejudice. Instead of managing conflict, we can become oppositional to a fault.

Moral certitude with the patina of faith is particularly danger-ous. Religious faith or activism based on spirituality without humility is destined to do harm. History is filled with people who conflated their religious beliefs with their ego's grandiose needs. In most of these cases, the individuals who eventually did great harm started out with the intention of doing a prodigious amount of good. Just because you have clarity in your motives does not excuse you from self-suspicion concerning personal prejudice and prideful assertion of only one path to a goal. We can be right and wrong at the same time.

Asking these questions: What if I am wrong? Is there a better way? Am I on the path of progress? Is a vulnerable activity. Yet, while these questions are essential, they can only be considered in a safe and supportive environment. This is the work of friends and trusted loved ones. These are people who will tell you the truth in direct, kind, and effective ways. Individualized spirituality often led to a projection of ego and prejudice. God moves through people as a means of moving people. Spiritual growth often parallels a deepening of the quality of relationships.

Ask yourself: To whom can I be vulnerable enough to ask hard questions and trust their answers? If you have no such people around, then you are only in dialogue with yourself. The voice of God is too closely identified with the sound of your own perspective. You need people. You need accountability. People who believe that they are connected to God but disconnected from other people are neither.

Courage

Call to Worship

WEEK FIVE

GOD, we gather in a time of selfishness and self-centeredness to seek you so that we can have an encounter with greater love.

In our worship, we seek to move past our weaponized faith, toxic politics, and sanctioned acceptance of language that bullies and belittles those who are different from us.

May our experience of your presence leave us with a bodacious spirit that will enable us to challenge violent words and actions that are used to hurt others. Embolden our voices to be advocates for the vulnerable. Inspire us to rise above our selfish desires to be popular. Break us of our insistence to assert our rights rather than to joyfully indulge in our human capacity to engage in self-sacrificing love and care for others.

Come with me and worship the God of a greater love that will upend our selfishness. Come with me and risk hearing the story of a mind-blowing experience of love that will not leave us the same. Come with me and lose your inhibitions about religion, relationships, and community. Come, let us worship anew and see what an encounter with God's love can do!

Valuing the Right Things

Week Five – Day One

"God, we gather in a time of selfishness and self-centeredness to seek you so that we can have an encounter with greater love. "

BETWEEN self-fulfillment and selfishness, there has always been a distinct line between compromise and self-sacrifice. Lately, that line has been crossed. Progress without sacrifice, accomplishments without delayed gratification, and asserting privileges as rights have become the perceived norm. The expectations of the measurements of success, such as the number of followers, size of crowds, volume of sales, size of salaries, and social media likes, have become oppressive and unrealistic measures of success.

It is truly astonishing that many people believe that the work of justice and peace will always lead to fame. In fact, the opposite, often, has been the case. Obscurity and scorn have been the rewards of many of the most effective social activists, preachers, prophets, and servants. The stories we know of them are among the few that have been told. Their stories have often been deleted or sanitized to hide the guilty from history.

It is a courageous decision to define success in terms of lifting others as you rise. It takes longer and is far more burdensome to move

59

people forward than to simply go forward on your own. It is easier to entertain than to educate. It is more wearying to lead people to rise to their most noble aspirations than to manipulate them to fall prey to their deepest fears. By this metric, you can be quite successful, but you can feel like a failure.

Don't forget the goal. Even if it is the right decision, it has never been an easy one. Because of the path you choose, others may scoff at your decision or, worse yet, pity you. You may hear, "You could have been and should have been more if you just didn't care about how things are done." But who were the beneficiaries of the wealth? What effect do actions and policies have on those who have the least?

Discouragement is a part of every journey and every life. Courage is created by what you choose to count. Love, hope, and justice are measured in lives saved, people who got up with your help, policies and policymakers who were challenged and changed by your witness, and relationships that were repaired by your kindness and forgiveness. The power of a "thank you" can fuel many new attempts at love. The testimony of a life touched by your efforts can illuminate dark times of discouragement. One change can remind you that change and miracles are possible.

Surprisingly, when you decide that these things count, they have a way of becoming more discernible. What you pay attention to is what you see the most. Astonishing love always surrounds us. The low rumble of hope is always in the background of discouragement.

Yes, the selfish and the self-centered are loud. However, because you are not in competition with them, their preening and boosting of their success can be endured. Your hope is for a shared future, not a selfish one. You want everyone to win.

Meanness, Anger and Lies

Week Five – Day Two

*"In our worship, we seek to move past our weaponized faith,
toxic politics, and sanctioned acceptance of language that
bullies and belittles those who are different from us."*

THE work of saints is done by human beings. In our humanness, we can be hurt, we can be wounded, and we can suffer debilitating pain that emotionally cripples us. Personal and mean-spirited attacks are not without effect. Though we try to ignore and deflect the words of hatred and bigotry, some nevertheless hit their targets in our minds and spirits. Our reaction to this is either our greatest victory or our worst defeat.

It is not that we did not expect opposition. But opposition is one thing; bullying, personal threats, and outright cruelty are quite another. In fact, no one can be prepared for the lies, taunts, and brutish laughter of people who seemingly are only focused on hurting and humiliating people. To them, nothing is off limits. Your family, friends, mistakes, and physical insecurities are in the bullseye of those whose agenda is to personalize their conflict with you. They belittle anyone who would dare to raise their voice for justice and peace. To these people, civility is a sign of weakness and a lack of commitment.

For those who value spirituality and faith as centers for our lives, it is particularly galling that faith and/or religion are being used as drivers of this approach. Besides creating a justification for cruelty, some "religious leaders" manipulate faith to create a fragile facade of supernatural meaning and purpose for meanness. These leaders manipulate religious texts and symbols of purity and evangelism to become a form of political sadism. They strip the awe out of worship in lieu of emotional manipulation—generating fear, false pride, and adoration for a leader. They suppose that salvation and change will come through their enemies' pain and humiliation. Of course, this is not the way to political or spiritual salvation. Nevertheless, they do have an effect.

As we fight for more love and freedom in the world, we often feel our sense of personal liberty shrinking. Your personal physical and emotional safety is affected. It is a human thing to want to respond. But the question is: How do you respond? The more energy you put into responding to these attacks, the worse their reaction will be. Their goal is to inflict pain and disrupt the lives of those upon whom they are focused. In the face of such fire, how does one suffocate it rather than fuel it?

You can't beat meanness, anger, and terror with the weapons of their warfare. Responding to insults in kind and arguing with those who do not value your humanity or recognize the validity of others who do not think like them is a useless and draining activity. Every reaction expands the perception that they are more powerful and numerous than they really are. A perception of influence and an inflated number of followers attracts those who feel powerless and invisible. Therein lies their real danger—a multiplication of power not by their intellectual prowess or physical numbers but by our reactions to them. Remember, their power is founded on lies.

Do not unwittingly become their megaphone. You have the right to defend yourself, but you would do well to not be defensive. Love is more powerful than hatred. It does, however, take longer to come to fruition. The path it takes is through healing, reconciliation, and redemption so that we can arrive together in a better place for all. That is not a straight line. Do not let the growling criticisms and attacks make you lose your focus. Remember the advice of John Lewis, *I happen to believe that God is love that love is God. Hate is too much of a burden to bear. If you start hating, in the end, how are you going to decide who you are going to hate today and love tomorrow? When you fail to accept the Christian doctrine of love and nonviolence as a way of life, as a way of living, and merely a tactic, it becomes like a faucet that you can turn on and off. Love in action, Christian love, is a better way, a more excellent way, and it's more redemptive. I don't know how to explain it, but I somehow came to that point, as I grew in my faith, that this is the way, this is the way out, and the way out is the way in.* (https://beatitudescenter.org/my-long-lost-conversation-on-nonviolence-with-john-lewis/)

Shout!

"Embolden our voices to be advocates for the vulnerable.
Inspire us to rise above our selfish desires to be popular.
Break us of our insistence to assert our rights rather
than to joyfully indulge in our human capacity to
engage in self-sacrificing love and care for others."

THE struggle for justice needs a voice. Silence is acquiescence. A whisper is noncommittal. A shout is what is needed to cut through the noise and steady drone of the ordinary. An authentic cry of outrage is necessary to be taken seriously and convey the importance of movement. Passion has a sound.

It is not surprising that people are always telling the victims, the protestors, and the advocates to tone it down. They try to convince us that the volume, not the content, of our objections and protests is the reason for some of the resistance to change. A polite and politically retrained tone, they argue, would serve us better. Consequently, those who are loud mouths of insistence are often vilified as the obstacles for change.

Unfortunately, this vilification is surprisingly more effective than it may first seem. No one, especially those of us who are advocating for hurting people and a devastated planet, want to be in the way of change and progress. For fear that such things are not productive, over time, you can find yourself stifling your raw and clear emotions. Those who want to protect the status quo can use your style and emotion as a wedge issue with your allies, telling them that they feel intimidated by the truth and emotion of your presence and witness.

To a lie, truth is intimidating. For the passive, outrage is uncomfortable. Your insistence on remembering the cost of injustice is jarring to those who are benefiting from the present system. You are told:

"Don't be so dramatic."

"It doesn't take all that."

"The stories are not as important as the policies."

"It is not helpful to talk about the problems all the time without knowing the solutions."

"Lived experiences are not as important as data points."

All such statements insinuate, "Shush. Be quiet and tone down!" There is an implied threat that you will not be taken seriously if you do not raise your issues in comfortable ways.

Remember that people rarely change because they see the light. They change because they feel the heat. Your passion is not only legitimate but also necessary. Your raw and emotional appeal of centering the hurting of people and the consequence of injustice is not in opposition to other forms of engagement; it is in support of immediate change. A loud cry is the result of empathy and compassion. Crying with those who are shedding tears and yelling for justice for the victims of historical and recent harms means that they are indeed being heard.

Faith and spirituality that are silent in the presence of hurt and pain are the definition of irrelevant. It is either magical hallucinations or escapism. Do not temper your voice. Be bold without being bitter. Be loud without arrogance. Be consistent without being obnoxious. This is the time for a bold witness. Inhale the breath of the spirit and exhale the voice of advocacy.

Passion has a sound.

Tell the Story

"Come with me and risk hearing the story of a mind-blowing experience of love that will not leave us the same."

TESTIMONIES are not only for the speaker. They are also for the hearers. Testimonies provide the north star of our work.

Issues do not have the same power to motivate, clarify, and inspire as do the stories of those who are affected by them. Simply because of the intrusion of the administrative and organizational work that must be done, one can become distant from the stories of the people and communities that you are fighting for.

Inadequate housing involves stories of people living on the streets and children growing up in unsafe places.

Amid the issue of global warming are the stories of people losing jobs and people dying of heat and cold in places that used to be easily habitable. Within racism are the stories of overqualified people not being hired.

The reality of overpolicing is reflected in the testimonies of poor and powerless people being killed by overworked, undertrained, and unaccountable bad police who leave children without parents, parents burying children, and otherwise law-abiding citizens being afraid of driving, walking, working, and living in their own communities.

Hidden behind the existence of Conversion therapy are the stories of religious organizations teaching parents that rejecting their kids is loving their kids and causing suicides and the destruction of their children because of their actions. Horrific and sadistic practices are meted out to vulnerable and frightened people with lifelong lingering effects of PTSD and self-hatred. Within the concept of prison reform are the stories of innocent people losing their lives and people who have grown through the experience of accountability not being given a chance to change their lives.

The consequences of sexism are heard in the stories of little girls who think that they are only good for breeding and cleaning, and of women who are not trusted to make their own decisions and thus accept abuse and neglect as the predetermined path of their gender.

The issues are numerous, and the stories are overwhelming. That is the point! Their presence reminds us that the issues have immediate points of pain in our fellow humans that must be addressed with urgency. Remind yourself and others of the stories of those affected by injustice, violence, and lack of opportunity. These tales of people's resiliency, as well as the sheer unfairness of the requirement that they be so, should always resound in your ears and beat in the depths of your heart. The testimonies also reveal the arc of progress that cannot be fully discerned at the macroscale.

Each person's story should remind us that while we are fighting to change whole systems, small changes can change lives. They are a measure of real change. Holding on to the experience of an impacted person can help clarify the question of who is being helped? Who is being harmed? How does this help someone live a better life now?

We need to keep the testimonies of people at the forefront of our work? Quite often, the people whose lives are most affected are not invited to the negotiating table. They are considered part of a larger narrative. In discussions of policy or system change, the decision-makers can be swept up in the thrill of the attainable solution, rather than the right solution. Budgets, financing, and political efficacy litter the vocabulary of change. While these are important, they must be balanced by intentionally keeping the lived experiences of those impacted top of mind.

Also, don't forget to allow yourself to listen to the stories of the difference you have made in others' lives. Do not dismiss yourself. You can be so captured by the frustrations of what hasn't changed that you can forget about the effect of your efforts on individuals whose lives have been made better by your actions. We want to save millions, but there is great value in saving one. Listen to the stories.

Do not allow the fear of being lulled into complacency or arrogance by the sounds of appreciation keep you from hearing the gratitude of others. Indeed, change work is a group effort. But that does not mean that your choices, sacrifices, and efforts should be dismissed. It can seem like an indulgence to accept praise. But, in fact, it is a necessary gift of strength. To downplay or dismiss words of appreciation disrespects those who took the time and effort to give them to you.

While you are in the business of letting others know how important they are, don't forget how critical you and the work that you do are to others. You are important to important people!

When things make no sense

Week Five – Day Five

"Come with me and lose your inhibitions about religion, relationships, and community. Come, let us worship anew and see what an encounter with God's love can do!"

GOD does not leave the work unfinished. Our awareness of the presence of God does. In this absence, we can become filled with the exhaustion of frustrated hope and the pain of failure. Richard Rohr wrote in his book, *What the Mystics Know: Seven Pathways to a Deeper Self,* "We cannot attain the presence of God because we are already in the presence of God. What is missing is awareness."

When we lose awareness, gone is the expectation of miracles, or at least the power of coincidence. There is the feeling that God called us into this work and then abandoned us in the work. Everyone experiences frustration. But for people of faith, frustration feels like abandonment. Worse yet, this feeling comes with a large dose of guilt. We have been conditioned to think that when we lose our awareness of God, it is because we are unfaithful.

There is a palpable pain and emotional cost to standing in the eye of the storm of criticism and mean-spirited attacks. There is a great flow of tears caused by dealing with irrational obstacles that are intentionally placed in the way of the most basic acts of kindness and decency. There is a lung crushing experience attached to meeting the unfair burdens of others' expectations of rapid change. Frankly, it is a lot.

Our faith did not shrink. Though the tendency, while you are in such a state, is to simply give in to despair and stop, remember that *God did not leave the work*. Our practice of faith and our intentions within it have been challenged by the experience and practice of our lives.

Within the work of justice and peace is the personal and collective work of adjusting and growing physically, socially, and psychologically. We know and celebrate this. We tout the goodness of change. We fight for change. We witness to others that God changes lives. Amid that, remember that you will be surprised by people. That is a good thing and a check on untethered ideals. Our ability to adapt and learn from our struggles is the genius of our humanity. We grow.

The divine does not have an obligation to act and behave in the way that you can understand. That is a rigid understanding of God. In such rigidity, we slowly lose our understanding of goodness and our advocacy of God. But if we stretch beyond our rigid definitions and perceptions, faith and adoration will increase to include the image of oneself and the community in partnership with the divine that one has always known.

When the world changes in ways that do not fit into the picture of what we believe are God's desires for the world, we can become fearful and oppositional. We are left with the quandary of trying to reconcile God's certainty and life's uncertainty. This is the work of spiritual growth. It begins when our notions of "what should be" are in opposition to "what is." It is stirred up when our verbal commitment to love people appears to be keeping us from the action of loving people. It is disconcerting and uncomfortable to hear that our advocacy for God is causing harm to those who are made in the image of God.

Think of a flashlight beam; it illumines what it is pointed at, but it leaves in the dark and unknown what it outside of that ray. In our work, we are that flashlight beam. In the work for justice and peace, we sweep the beam from side to side, illuminating and understanding the unfamiliar. When we do so, we know that we shine light on that which depends on our blindness—systems and structures that harm our fellow humans. The outcome is that our awareness of God, our notions of the actions and reactions of God, and a growing connection with the divine push us to challenge the human pain, suffering, and inequality around us.

The power and presence of God are constants, whether you fully feel, understand, or see God. Do not be afraid. You are not having a crisis of faith. You are involved in the work of faith. You are teaming with the spirit of creation. God is not scared, and neither should you be. What is changing is our experience and understanding of God. Worship anew and see what love can do when it is unleashed in us and works through us without the inhibitions of conformity.

Again, I wonder:

When did acts of meanness become pranks?

When did self-promotion become marketing?

When did civility become a sign of weakness and a reason to question one's radical bona fides? (Liberal or Conservative)

When did being in someone's presence stop necessarily meaning that you were present with them? (Texting and surfing on the phone)

When did people think standing up for one's faith means standing on someone's rights?

Since when did the church become so self-aggrandizing as to believe that the government or the society was supposed to believe what it believes simply because it believes it?

When did the success of Christianity become measured by the ballot box instead of the altar?

When did facts stop being important?

"What in the World?"

Call to Worship

WEEK SIX

DAZED by the dizzying distractions of life, we come to you for focus, clarity, and calmness. Forgive us for our tendency to focus on the tasks of life rather than the purpose of life.

We seek to luxuriate in your presence and bask in your love without doubting our worthiness for either of these. We gather to celebrate and remember the way that you love us—without condemnation and with total forgiveness.

In accepting your forgiveness, may we discover forgiveness for the ways that we have disappointed ourselves and learn to offer forgiveness to others who have disappointed us.

Empower us to bestow love lavishly and courageously on others. Let our wells of grace rise in us until they overflow in gratitude and overflow the banks of tradition and conventional wisdom.

So, we bow, pray and praise with the hope that we will be changed by the experience of being with you and become more like the people you created us to be. Come, let us worship in spirit and see the truth!

Focus

Week Six – Day One

*"Dazed by the dizzying distractions of life we come to you
for focus, clarity, and calmness. Forgive us for our tendency
to focus on the tasks of life rather than the purpose of life."*

AT every moment in history, the following statements have been made:

The world is on fire.

The apocalypse is about to happen.

Governments are imploding.

War is breaking out all over the globe.

People are angry.

It is truly astonishing that we human beings have not managed our own annihilation. But it has not been for lack of trying.

For many of us, we have come to the realization that one of our most important functions is holding space for the hurting and the under-represented. We know that change will not come soon enough for its present victims. This is the intimate work of an advocate. To simply listen, to dry the eyes of the crying, and to validate the pain of the victim. It is of immense importance to make sure that people have a safe emotional, psychological, and physical space to grieve, yell, and heal from the effects of the experience of evil.

We listen to the needs of the people with whom and for whom we work. Sometimes, people just need a break from fighting. Sometimes, the greater goal is not more important than the healing of the present pain; assuring people that they do not have to be noble is important. We have to find a way to be at peace with the "already but not yet" of life and struggle. Otherwise, we can become driven by crises instead of our hearts.

To create this space means that we must overcome our own sense of loss and failure. It is an occupational hazard for those continually dealing with a world in crisis to carry tension and anxiety in their body and soul. It is to be in a flight or fight mode. The media, our personal conversations, and the personal attacks of those in opposition can rob us of our peace. Human beings cannot stay in a continuous state of conflict and agitation without doing great harm to themselves.

Faith is a renewal of focus on the power of love, renewal, and the miraculous over the immediate conditions of the struggle. Take a moment to remember what victory looks like. It is not simply policy changes, reparations, and new laws. It is a grounding of being with the divine AND one another. It is the ability to find connection and collaboration in the midst of conflict. This is an intentional and disciplined act of focus. In many faith traditions, this is the function of prayer. It is the practice of meditation. These are the practices that expand our spiritual capacity and strength to hold space for others and healthy spaces for ourselves.

Let us pray:

Open the eyes of our hearts and the windows of our souls to flood us with the light of grace and love. Expand our perceptions of matter and energy to make us open to the enormity of the ways and means that God act in us, around us and through us. Connect us with the possibility and power of our collective humility.

Mistakes, Memories
and Motivation

Week Six – Day Two

*"We seek to luxuriate in your presence and bask in your
love without doubting our worthiness for either of these.
We gather to celebrate and remember the way that you love
us – without condemnation and with total forgiveness."*

WHEN we retire for the night and seek the shelter of sleep, the various
accusations of our critics are easily dismissed. We know the truth of our
own lives. Rather, we must confront our worst critic and most unrelent-
ing nightmare—our own self-critical voice of regret. The solitude of the
night lets in self-doubt and chases away the bravado of confidence that
we broadcast in our struggles for others. At that moment, we are alone
to ponder our role in the disappointments and frustrations of the day.
Sometimes, we can admit to ourselves that we could have been better.
We should have done more. We let people down. We were not able to
deliver the results that were needed. We were not as courageous in the
moment as we should have been.

The most painful disappointment that we can suffer is with ourselves. Worst of all, such regrets and disappointments are inevitable. The human experiences of ignorance, cowardice, or plain bad judgment all periodically invade our days and haunt our nights. Our friends and foes alike seem to delight in our mistakes, lapses of integrity, or inconsistency as witnesses. For fear of their manipulation of our stumbles, we do not take the time to heal from the wounds of our falls. Thus, the scars and hurts of our self-inflicted wounds fester and change us.

We begin to walk and act differently in the world. Our ability to be vulnerable or to listen diminishes, and our isolation increases. If we stop to examine ourselves, we fear that we would be overwhelmed by a doubt that would lead to hesitancy. That, we fear, would be worse than the mistakes that we have made. When we push forward amidst this, people experience us as self-righteous and stubborn; what they are in fact seeing is self-protection or guardedness.

Accept the fact that we will mess-up; purity is a false and onerous expectation. Others will put great effort into making these moments painful and embarrassing. But they are not the arbitrators of your truth. Your faith and experience of the divine are the light in which you stand. You don't need to explain yourself. You cannot you protect yourself from the volume of the gloating attacks. You can, however, retreat under the shelter of your experience of a loving God who created us with foibles and who is neither surprised nor stymied by our lapses in consistency. In this, we will find a safe retreat from our condemnation of our own ability to be co-opted by the very system and evils with which we are contending.

Faith does not excuse anyone from accountability; on the contrary, it challenges people to take responsibility to do better. Because you are a person of faith, you should believe in the certainty of your ability to rise above yourself and trust in the presence of grace. Remember that forgiveness is the path to the future, not only for others but also for yourself. Let others cry that you are not worthy of your cause. Let them say that you do not deserve to be heard.

Embrace your weakness. Learn from it. It is the connection to our common human experience. No one is perfect. When we fall and get back up again, we are wiser and stronger. Know that as we learn, forgive, and change, we lead in the struggle for our fellow human beings to do so. Rest up and rise again with a determination to continue the process of inspiring change in the world and encouraging us to love one another. Let's keep practicing love until we get it right!

A great cloud of witnesses

*"Let our wells of grace rise in us until they overflow in gratitude
to overflow the banks of tradition and conventional wisdom."*

AS quiet as it is, one of the most important reasons that we engage in this difficult work is gratitude. We are indebted to the people who gifted us their stories and transparently shared their pain, frustrations, and journeys to their own insights. Some of these people—teachers, workers, family members, and friends—went out of their way to find us and get our attention. Some of them told their stories as confessions of regret. Others shared themselves as a means of creating value in their own lives. Some simply allowed us to walk beside them. We observed them as they experienced the frustrations and injustice of struggling for their lives, liberty, and happiness with systems and people who intentionally or unintentionally denied them their equal rights.

People do not emerge into communities with the knowledge, passion, and insight that are needed to work for justice and peace in the world. Such things come from formative experiences and relationships. Many of these were surprising and unpredictable. We would not be who we are without a loving connection with others who invaded our space and convinced us that we and the world could be better together. Indeed, they revealed that we are better than we thought we were.

This gratitude is a powerful force. It is an amazing motivator. Our work is a monument to these people, who have become our mentors. Appreciation also provides a ballast to our work. Our highs of achievement and our lows of losses are contextualized in a broader narrative than just our own stories. We realize that we are fulfilling other's dreams and creating new dreams, that we will not ourselves see come to fruition, for those who will follow. Our gratitude creates a perspective of a community not bound by time but by intentions, prayers, and hope.

Take time to stop and remember those who brought you into this fellowship of hopeful and persevering people. Even death could not stop the force of their fierce love for justice. They bequeathed it to you. They mentored you for a future that they would never experience. Take the time to pen a note, text, email, or phone call to those who now inspire you. Let yourself feel the force of that gratitude. Yes, you are forging new roads; but you are also walking pathways that have been carved through the hard rocks of resistance by past generations.

Already and not yet – Regarding History

Week Six – Day Four

"...until they overflow in gratitude to overflow the banks of tradition and conventional wisdom."

THERE is a thin line between respect for history and resistance to change. Gratitude can turn into pride. Pride can become a heritage. Heritage can become tradition. Tradition can become an obstacle to change. The width of this line can be measured by the length of time that it takes between an innovative thought and a courageous action. Because of this, we are all susceptible to this slippery slope of being captive to history instead of catapulted to change.

The chains of complacency become fastened to our thoughts and choices by a false comparison of the results of the past without regard to the internal struggles. Almost everyone whom we now consider an historically significant person was controversial among their peers. They were viewed with suspicion and sometimes fear. They often challenged the conventional wisdom with their strategies for change. Their actions and accomplishments are remembered, but the conflicts and internal struggles with their peers, elders, and community have either been forgotten or intentionally recast as creative tension. Because of this, one can find oneself dismissing ideas and strategies that are not "respectful" of the history of the struggle.

Innovation and bold assertion are the real legacies of those who preceded us in the struggles for justice and peace. Walking in this legacy and history, the road to healing, hope, and justice not only is not a straight line but also often takes new forms of transportation. It is not disrespectful to adjust the language, leadership, or even the goals of movements that were products of their times. In fact, you have a responsibility to consider again what you are called to do. Respect is being open to challenging the conventional wisdom, both from those with whom we are in conflict and those with whom we are in partnership. History is a guide, but it is not a straight jacket.

Respecting elders and history while being true to your own sense of calling and vision can be emotionally difficult. You may be accused of being unappreciative of the past struggles. It is important to pause and consider the accusations. Something can be not quite true, but it is still important because of what it reveals about those who utter and/or believe it. The past is not a millstone. However, we must accept that it is a weight that we must carry in order to retain our balance. Completely disavowing or disregarding the past is not wise. To be interrogated by the past is to become a better witness in the present.

The times do change, but humans remain eerily the same. The histories of all cultures and people reveal our shared struggle with power, privilege, ignorance, and evil. The tactics have been consistent: gaslighting, lying, use of violence, and disruption, to name a few. Generational knowledge is not necessary to maintain the status quo. The continuation of the relationships that have created the systems of inequality, injustice, and environmental disaster have been perpetuated and supported. However, it is essential that the stories and experiences of the successes and failures of those contending against this system are shared; they are encouragement, and we strive to turn.

The function of sacred and spiritual texts is to challenge us and to interrogate us as to our fidelity to our faith and vision of the world. Continue in dialogue with the tension of the past and the insights into the present. This conversation is part of the alchemy of wisdom. It gives context to our struggles, depth to our feelings, and broadens our lived experience, joining us in an intergenerational longing to be better. Stop and read history, talk with, and listen to past leaders. Learn what was conventional, and then be confident in your response to the present calling of this generation.

Encourage Yourself

*"...So, we bow, to pray and praise with the hope that
we will be changed by the experience of being with you
to become more like who you created us to be."*

INEVITABLY, this work changes you in unpredictable ways. Constantly
being in tension-filled relationship with people who are doing their
best or worse influences who we are and who we become. Only the
woefully unconscious could become a part of this enterprise without
experiencing some self-doubt, critical dissonance, or a re-examination
of every relationship in one's life.

Every disappointment causes rifts in our hope and challenges
our faith in God and our fellow human beings. Anger, resignation, and
exhaustion are always eroding our resolve. We are in a constant state
of repair and rebuild of our physical, mental, and spiritual well-being.

It is a wise and necessary expenditure of our energy to encourage
ourselves and connect to our sources of spiritual energy and imagination. We are always re-digging our wells, if we fail to dig deeper than our
immediate experiences and feelings, we will soon hit the bottom of our

resources. Simply put, what is being taken from us must be replenished. Otherwise, we will have nothing left for ourselves and will offer nothing.

The joyful surprise is that within the process of examining ourselves, pondering the connections with our community (both living and dead), and discovering the inexplicable power of human beings to persevere against any rational expectations to do so, we are changed. We discover vistas of courage and humility that were previously hidden behind the minutia of trivial details and buried under petty hurts. We are given evidence of lived experiences and testimonies of the fact of miracles. We are encouraged by our encounters with truth that although human beings can be prodigiously cruel, they can also be powerfully merciful and kind. We discovered that redemption is possible, all lives matter, and love is hard and complex.

The internal life of our emotions must make choices. We will rise to meet the challenges of this experience by expanding our beliefs and commitment to joy and hope. Or we will recoil and shrink into a small space of cynicism and despair. Our work can bolster us to be stronger than we ever imagined.

The Christian notion of discipleship is the work of making the world better and helping our communities become more equitable and inclusive, this is how we become what we were created to be. The purpose of our existence and the meaning of our lives is an intentional act of human beings mentoring each other from one generation to another. Each generation absorbs, rejects, and makes its own relationship with the divine; then it shares the process with the next. In so doing, this process makes us better because it gives us the optimistic certainty that we can and will do better. No one mentors another with the words, "Your life is destined to fail, and the world will not get better." Rather, the work of mentorship is to instill hope and inspire optimism. If one mentors another only in words and not in action, the outcome is personal failure and communal stagnation or regression. Rather, through a mentorship of intention and action, the pathos of life is shared with and influences the ethos of the future.

Focus on your call, not as a creation of your time, but as an eternal legacy for the future. Even if the change you are fighting for is slow, your example and integrity provide the light to pathways that others will walk to achieve the shared goals. Our all-too-few moments of time are dwarfed by the specter of eternity.

Our lives, however, have meaning and purpose that will cast a light far into a future that is more than the promise of our individual existence. Live well and fiercely. Even if you are convinced some days that you will not change the world in which you live, you will indeed change the world!

Thank you for purchasing and reading this book.
If you enjoyed this book, please write a review on Amazon.
Tell someone about your experience and
share it with someone. You are invited to
check out the author's other books.